BOOK THREE
BASED ON THE HIT TV SHOW 'THE AVENGERS'

STEED and Mrs PEEL

ILLUSTRATED BY
IAN GIBSON

WRITTEN BY
GRANT MORRISON · THE GOLDEN GAME
ANNE CAULFIELD · DEADLY RAINBOW

ECLIPSE BOOKS · ACME COMICS

STEED AND Mrs PEEL Book Three

Published by
Eclipse Comics,
P.O. Box 1099, Forestville, California 95436 USA
and
Acme Comics, 391 Coldharbour Lane, London SW9 8LQ UK.

Writers:
Grant Morrison
Anne Caulfield
Artist:
Ian Gibson
Letterer:
Ellie de Ville
Designer:
Rian Hughes
Editor:
Dick Hansom
Back Cover Photographer:
John R Ward
Consulting Editors:
Dave Rogers
Catherine Yronwode
Michael Bennent

"An Elephant Never Forgets"
Titheradge/Schumann/Griffiths/Elkin
© Ascherberg, Hopwood and Crew
Reproduced by Warner Chappell Music Ltd.

Eclipse Comics:
Dean Mullaney, Publisher
Catherine Yronwode, Editor-In-Chief
Jan Mullaney, Chairman
Bruce Palley, Vice-President
Ted Adams, Circulation
Beau Smith, Sales Manager

Acme Press Editorial Board:
Richard Ashford
Katey Bird
Dick Hansom
Cefn Ridout

ISBN 1-870084-96-9

Printed in the USA.

part four:

DID WE **GET** HER?

I DON'T KNOW, DO I? I'M NOT **PSYCHIC**, AM I?

ANYWAY, IF WE DIDN'T GET HER BEFORE, WE'LL DEFINITELY GET HER **NOW**.

JUST BE **CAREFUL** THERE.

I HAD A TUSSLE WITH HER WHEN I WAS DOING THE **GRAVE-DIGGER** BIT FOR THE GUV'NOR.

SHE'S NO **PUSH-OVER**.

STILL, WE **MUST** HAVE GOT HER.

I DIDN'T SEE HER GETTING OUT.

WILL YOU SHUT UP FOR JUST ONE...

AAH!

RIGHT.

LET'S NOT WASTE TIME ON INTRODUCTIONS.

WHERE'S JOHN STEED?

NEED A HAND?

WHY, MRS PEEL! FANCY MEETING YOU HERE.

I'M YOUR 'GET OUT OF JAIL FREE' CARD, STEED.

PITY ABOUT THE UMBRELLA.

I PROMISE I'LL BUY YOU A NEW ONE WHEN WE GET OUT.

COMING?

THE PALAMEDES CLUB MEMBERS ARE STILL OUT THERE SOMEWHERE.

YES, I KNOW.

80

81

82

83

HURRF

OHHH

HKKK

HELLO AGAIN.

YOU'VE LOST WEIGHT.

I TRY TO EXERCISE.

ANYONE FOR TENNIS?

AAAH!

PASS THE PARCEL, MRS PEEL!

IF YOU INSIST.

YOUR SERVE, HILARY?

NO, WAIT. I JUST...

THE END

STEED?

AH, GOOD. AT LEAST YOU DIDN'T SAY, 'WHERE AM I?'

I KNOW EXACTLY WHERE I AM... WHAT I WANT TO KNOW IS HOW I GOT HERE.

OH, IT WAS JUST ANOTHER HEROIC RESCUE ON MY PART...

AND WHERE'S MY HUSBAND?

YOUR HUSBAND? HMMM... DO YOU THINK HE'S AN AWFULLY GOOD INFLUENCE, MRS PEEL?

WHAT ON EARTH DO YOU MEAN BY THAT?

OH, NOTHING REALLY... IT'S JUST THAT I STROLLED INTO THE CHURCH WONDERING WHERE ALL THE VILLAGERS HAD GOT TO...

...AND FOUND YOU STRAPPED TO THE ALTAR, SCREAMING AND BARELY CONSCIOUS.

YOU DIDN'T BEHAVE LIKE THAT WHEN YOU WERE WITH ME.

DON'T BLAME MY HUSBAND... BLAME THE INCA VICAR AND THE LITTLE PEOPLE.

INCA VICAR?... LITTLE PEOPLE?... JUST HOW STRONG IS THE LOCAL BREW?

I'LL SHOW YOU...

DIDN'T YOU NOTICE THESE STRANGE WINDOWS?

YES. STRANGE, BUT RATHER JOLLY REALLY.

AND THE VICAR WAS DRESSED IN RED LEATHER GLOVES AND...

THE CHURCH OF ENGLAND ISN'T WHAT IT WAS...

BUT I ASSURE YOU, APART FROM YOU ON THE ALTAR, THE PLACE WAS ENTIRELY DESERTED WHEN I ARRIVED.

THOSE LOOK LIKE...

FILM CONTAINERS... CAMERA FILM CONTAINERS AND WRAPPINGS. THIS IS ALL GETTING HIDEOUSLY CONFUSING...

AND WHAT ARE YOU DOING HERE ANYWAY, STEED?

LET'S CALL ON THE VICAR FOR TEA. I'LL EXPLAIN ON THE WAY.

IF YOU PROMISE TO TELL ME, IN DETAIL, ABOUT THE VICAR'S RED LEATHER GLOVES...

Panel 1: OF COURSE I REMEMBER, MRS PEEL. IT'S BEEN ABSOLUTE AGES, BUT PEOPLE OFTEN TELL ME MY MEMORY IS REMARKABLE...

BUT YOU SAW ME THIS MORNING.

Panel 2: I'M SORRY, YOU MUST BE MISTAKEN...

I DON'T SUPPOSE YOU REMEMBER SEEING MY HUSBAND THIS MORNING EITHER...

MRS PEEL, UNTIL YOU WALKED IN HERE WITH THIS GENTLEMAN, I HADN'T SEEN YOU FOR SEVEN YEARS.

TELL ME VICAR, WHAT'S THE CONNECTION BETWEEN THIS VILLAGE AND THE INCA LEOPARD PEOPLE?

WHAT ARE YOU TALKING ABOUT, MY DEAR? THIS IS SLEEPY PRINGLE ON SEA...

NOTHING EVER HAPPENS HERE.

THEN WHAT'S IN THIS...?

25

27

YOU'RE BEING FRIGHTFULLY HASTY, MRS PEEL... WHY DON'T YOU TRY OPENING ANOTHER BOX?

COME ON STEED, HURRY...!

DO YOU THINK HE'LL BE IN THE CRYPT...

...OR UP THE SPIRE, STEED...?

STEED?!

JUST STAY WHERE YOU ARE, STEED...

...I'LL BE BACK AS SOON AS I CAN.

THERE SEEMS TO BE A BIT OF TROUBLE...

29

WELL, FAIR ENOUGH. OBVIOUSLY IT DOESN'T REVERSE... BUT DOES IT **STOP**?

THERE! OF COURSE IT STOPS. I THINK I'M GETTING THE HANG OF THIS...

OI! YOU!

LOOK WHAT YOU DONE TO THE GREENHOUSE! THAT SORT OF THING GIVES US A BAD NAME!

WHAT HAVE YOU DONE TO POOR BERT?

HE'S BETTER THAN HE WAS. AND SO ARE YOU...

...LAST TIME I SAW YOU LOT, YOU WERE THE SIZE OF **PINS**.

YOU THINK WE DON'T **KNOW** THAT? WHAT ARE WE -- **STUPID**?

YOU THINK WE DIDN'T **NOTICE** WE'D BEEN SHRUNK AND PUT IN A BOX?

IT'S CERTAINLY NOT THE SORT OF THING WE'RE USED TO, AND WE'RE WALKING OFF THIS JOB **RIGHT NOW**!

IF I WERE YOU I'D RUN!

BERT WON'T MAKE IT!

O.K. BERT, I OWE YOU A FAVOUR...

STEED! LISTEN TO ME!

SILENCE, IN THE NAME OF THE LEOPARD PEOPLE!

ALL RIGHT THEN... DON'T LISTEN.

32

YOU'RE NOT THE LEOPARD PEOPLE! WHO ARE YOU? WHAT HAVE YOU DONE TO STEED?

AND WHERE'S MY HUSBAND?

RETURN MY MATCH-BOXES AND I'LL SHOW YOU YOUR HUSBAND.

THE EFFECTS SHOULD BE WEARING OFF BY NOW ANYWAY.

BUT LET'S SPEED UP THE PROCESS.

PEEL! YOU'RE SAFE!

THE CONTENTS OF THIS ONE AREN'T SO IMPORTANT.

COME ON! WE'RE RUNNING LATE!

THIS ISN'T A BLASTED VICARAGE TEA PARTY!

INTERESTING, ISN'T IT? WE HAVE THE OPTION OF TOTAL SHRINKAGE-- A NEAT AND CONVENIENT WAY TO HOLD PEOPLE HOSTAGE...

...OR WE CAN MAKE THEM 'LEOPARD PEOPLE' SIZE. AND THEN OF COURSE ...

WE CAN MAKE THEM THINK LEOPARD THOUGHTS ...

WE CAN JUST KEEP CHOPPING AND CHANGING PEOPLE DEPENDING ON WHAT WE WANT FROM THEM...

... AND WE'RE DETERMINED TO GET WHAT WE WANT.

BRAINWASH

SHRINK

HALF-SHRINK

REVERSE

STEED!... PEEL!

SILENCE! TAKE A GOOD LOOK, MRS PEEL. THIS IS THE LAST YOU'LL SEE OF... **ONE** OF THEM!

YOU HAVE AN INTERESTING CHOICE, MRS PEEL...

AS THE STEAMROLLERS START TO MOVE FORWARD, YOU CAN USE THIS TO CUT FREE EITHER YOUR HUSBAND OR JOHN STEED.

BUT IF YOU TRY TO BE CLEVER AND SAVE **BOTH** OF THEM...

...WE WILL **KILL** BOTH OF THEM! AH, GOOD...

...OUR **GUESTS** HAVE ARRIVED!

THE PRESS?!

FULL STEAM AHEAD!

HOOT!

36

STOP!

YOUR DAY OF SAFE PASSAGE IS OVER. NOW, FLEE FOR YOUR LIVES!

WHAT YOU HAVE SEEN IS ONLY A WARNING...

GO ... AND TELL THE WORLD THAT THE REVENGE OF THE LEOPARD PEOPLE IS JUST BEGINNING!

NEWS

EXPRESS

Mrs Peel Vs Inca Priest

True Face of the Leopard People

...man ...crifice

Leopard Terror in Pringle

Leopard People Show their Spots

Torture and Terror

Jungle Savages

Peel's Leopard People are Monsters

STEED? MRS PEEL? LEOPARD PEOPLE?

WHY THE DICKENS DOES NO ONE TELL ME WHAT'S GOING ON?

NOW, LET'S CUT YOU DOWN TO SIZE...

TAKE THEM TO THE VICARAGE. THEY'LL BE USEFUL HOSTAGES.

WELL, OBVIOUSLY THEY'RE NOT PLANNING TO STARVE US TO DEATH.

BUT IT'S ALL SO TERRIBLY FATTENING... I HOPE THEY MOVE US TO A SALAD BOWL TOMORROW.

IT'S THE...

FIFTH! THERE'S NO TIME TO LOSE...

EMMA, WHERE ON EARTH ARE YOU GOING?

DON'T WORRY ABOUT THE EARTH -- JUST KEEP YOUR EYES ON THE SUN.

WHADDA WE DO ABOUT THE HOSTAGES?

THINK OF A REAL NASTY WAY TO KILL 'EM, SO THE LEOPARD PEOPLE GET BLAMED.

ANY MINUTE NOW, OR YOU'RE IN A LOT OF TROUBLE, MRS PEEL...

THE CONTROL CRYSTAL -- ONE OF THE HOSTAGES GOT TO IT!

I'LL CRUSH THAT VARMINT LIKE A TERMITE!

CRUSH ME IF YOU CAN FIND ME, BOYS!

WHERE'S THE DAYLIGHT GONE?

42

WHAT ARE YOU THINKING?

I'M WONDERING WHERE WE SHOULD PUT THOSE AMERICANS TO MAKE A GOOD PICTURE FOR THE NEWSPAPERS.

YES, THAT LOOKS VERY STRIKING... WHAT NEXT, PEEL?

BACK TO THE REAL LEOPARD PEOPLE IN BOLIVIA...

WHERE WE CAN SORT OUT THE REST OF THESE DIABOLICAL MASTERMINDS.

WHY DON'T YOU COME WITH US, STEED? YOU'D BE VERY USEFUL.

HOW NICE OF YOU, BUT THE JUNGLE ISN'T REALLY MY KIND OF THING.

THERE IS ONE THING PUZZLES ME. YOU SEE, BEFORE I CAME HERE, I LOOKED UP SOME LOCAL HISTORY MYSELF... AND THE TOTAL ECLIPSE ISN'T DUE TO HAPPEN UNTIL THE SEVENTH.

AH WELL, THE LEADER OF THE REAL LEOPARD PEOPLE MAY NOT RUN TO MIND CONTROL AND SHRINKAGE...

...BUT THEN AGAIN, HE'S FULL OF SURPRISES!"

I HATE TO MENTION THIS, BUT BOLIVIA IS COMPLETELY LAND-LOCKED-- WHY ARE YOU TAKING A SHIP OUT THERE?

LAST TIME I FLEW IN A PLANE, THE JOURNEY TOOK THREE YEARS.

THE SHIP AND A ROUTE MARCH THROUGH THE JUNGLE IS MUCH QUICKER...

A ROUTE MARCH? JUST DROP ME OFF AT CALAIS AND SEND ME A POSTCARD!

WHY DO I FEEL HURT THAT MRS PEEL MARRIED SOMEONE AS UNLIKE ME AS SHE COULD FIND?

THE END.